SUZANNE CAPORAEL

WHAT FOLLOWS HERE

525 West 22nd Street New York NY 10011
tel 212 445 0051 www.amy-nyc.com

What Does Abstraction Represent?
The Art of Suzanne Caporael

by Carter Ratcliff

In *710 (Glacier to lake)*, a painting from 2016, Suzanne Caporael places five forms in an immediately graspable configuration. What I see in the first moment is startlingly clear. Subsequent moments bring further, subtler clarities. I see how firmly the painting's grayish-blue forms are anchored by their architecture to the right-angled surface of the canvas, and how precisely the green form reaches in from the left to meet the acute angle of the "roof." Cued by allusions to built form and landscape—and by the painting's title—I read expanses of white as surfaces of water or ice, or as depths of sky. To reflect on these ambiguities is to arrive at other readings. Looking transforms this painting.

710 (Glacier to lake)'s allusions to architecture may find echoes in *709 (The widow's mite)* (2016) and *725 (The sign says you are here)* (2016). There is a watery landscape to be seen in *719 (D. Balmori island)* (2016). Yet, we could see these paintings as abstract, and it would be difficult to assign subject matter to the other works on view here.

Leaning, it would seem, toward unqualified abstraction, Caporael's art recalls a discussion that began late in the 19th century with speculations about "pure painting"—a phrase the Neo-Impressionist Paul Sérusier used in praise of Paul Cézanne.

By 1919, it was possible for Theo van Doesburg—one of the founders, with Piet Mondrian, of De Stijl—to talk of "colors, forms, lines, and planes" in a "pure state," uncompromised by any reference to the world's particulars. As van Doesburg saw it, abstraction revealed "the absolute equilibrium of the universe." Evoking the essence of all that is, painting is visual metaphysics. At the opposite pole is abstract painting that offers an image of the painter's essence: pure self-expression. It is a sign of Caporael's originality that she belongs nowhere on the continuum that connects these extremes.

Not that Caporael is absent from her art. The certainty of her line is legible as a personal as well as a pictorial quality, as is the elegance with which she outlines and interlocks her strips and blocks of color. Yet, her paintings have a dignity that makes it difficult to see her as an expressionist eager to broadcast her immediate feelings. Rather, she draws our attention to the self-evident justness of color-planes aligned precisely to the surface of the canvas and to the logicality of juxtaposing shapes in configurations that echo that surface's squared-away shape.

Caporael tempts us to conclude that she is, after all, a "pure" painter of an especially austere kind: a formalist whose forms refer only to themselves and to the surfaces on which they appear. But the temptation fades as departures from this formalist agenda make themselves felt.

See, for example, how the curving edge of the strip of darkness on the left-hand side of *724 (Stammer, sidewalk)* (2016) puts it into an endlessly ambiguous relationship with the surface it occupies. Its upper part reiterates the geometry of the surface, while the lower part floats free. So we could read into this presence the insurmountable contradictions of individuality: Each of us is a function of an environment, defined in ways we cannot control, and at the same time each of us is an independent being.

Caporael fills her art with occasions for symbolic readings of this kind. If we didn't know the title of *714 (Sun, moon, kiss, eclipse)* (2016), we might still see in this painting an image of light overtaken by darkness. Even with the title in mind, however, it is plausible to see light triumphant here. The instability of symbols makes them fecund. Caporael offers, in addition, rich possibilities for meaning in details not so much of form but of formal relationship.

4

Inflecting rectangular shapes with notches, angles, and curves, the artist dismantles the picture plane and opens her images to spatial ambiguity and intimations of time. Thus, she raises questions of proximity and juxtaposition, of connection and transition—contingencies that comprise our immediate environment and make it not merely inhabitable but also intelligible. Here, Caporael moves from symbol to representation, for she has invented a pictorial repertory that focuses the generalizing, synthesizing power of abstraction, not on metaphysical absolutes but on the shifting, enveloping world that we experience from moment to moment.

Of course, I see the contradiction in what I'm saying. Abstraction and representation are opposites. An abstract painting can't be representational. True, but that truth holds only on the plane of concepts. To respond to Caporael's paintings is to go beyond the reach of concepts to a realm of experience that is visual and implicitly physical, a zone where the meaning of a non-referential, non-figurative form can have the specificity usually found only in figurative painting.

How can this be? Answers to this question will emerge from the contemplative observation the artist encourages with her calm but invigorating colors. And our answers will take the form of visual intuitions, which is to say that they will always resist our attempts to articulate them. It is, nonetheless, possible to make this astonishing point: Caporael's abstract paintings picture our world—not its particular places but, rather, the structural details that make it possible for places to have their particularity in the first place. ■

* A note on sources: Paul Sérusier's comment on Paul Cézanne is quoted in Maurice Denis, "Cézanne," translated by Roger Fry, *Burlington Magazine*, January 1910, p. 214. Theo van Doesburg presented his theory of abstract painting in "Principles of Neo-Plastic Art" (1925), translated by Janet Seligman and reprinted in Charles Harrison and Paul Wood, eds., *Art in Theory 1900-2000: An Anthology of Changing Ideas*. Oxford: Blackwell Publishing, 2003, pp. 282–83.

Carter Ratcliff is a poet and art critic. A contributing editor to *Art in America*, his writing has appeared in major journals in the United States and abroad, and in catalogues published by the Museum of Modern Art, New York; the Guggenheim Museum, New York; the Royal Academy of Arts, London; and the Stedelijk Museum, Amsterdam. Ratcliff's books include *The Fate of a Gesture: Jackson Pollock and Postwar American Art; Out of the Box: The Reinvention of Art, 1965 - 1975*; monographs on John Singer Sargent, Georgia O'Keeffe, and Francis Bacon; and a novel, *Tequila Mockingbird*. His most recent book of poetry is *Arrivederci, Modernismo*.

706 (Poplar archive)

709 (*The widow's mite*)

710 (Glacier to lake)

711 (Hush, mute)

712 (Every autumn beyond counting)

713 (Sitka eddy)

714 (Sun, moon, kiss, eclipse)

716 (Slide Mountain dandelion)

717 (Blue almanac)

718 (The ploughman's line)

719 (D. Balmori island)

720 (Read the spill)

721 (*The days' noise*)

722 (Portage, noun or verb)

724 (Stammer, sidewalk)

725 *(The sign says you are here)*

PLATE LIST

page 7
706 (Poplar archive), 2016
Oil on linen
30 x 22 inches
76.2 x 55.9 cm

page 9
709 (The widow's mite), 2016
Oil on linen
30 x 22 inches
76.2 x 55.9 cm

page 11
710 (Glacier to lake), 2016
Oil on linen
30 x 22 inches
76.2 x 55.9 cm

page 13
711 (Hush, mute), 2016
Oil on linen
30 x 22 inches
76.2 x 55.9 cm

page 15
712 (Every autumn beyond counting), 2016
Oil on linen
30 x 22 inches
76.2 x 55.9 cm

page 17
713 (Sitka eddy), 2016
Oil on linen
30 x 22 inches
76.2 x 55.9 cm

page 19
714 (Sun, moon, kiss, eclipse), 2016
Oil on linen
30 x 22 inches
76.2 x 55.9 cm

page 21
716 (Slide Mountain dandelion), 2016
Oil on linen
30 x 22 inches
76.2 x 55.9 cm

page 23
717 (Blue almanac), 2016
Oil on linen
66 x 48 inches
167.6 x 121.9 cm

page 25
718 (The ploughman's line), 2016
Oil on linen
48 x 66 inches
121.9 x 167.6 cm

page 27
719 (D. Balmori island), 2016
Oil on linen
60 x 90 inches
152.4 x 228.6 cm

page 29
720 (Read the spill), 2016
Oil on linen
60 x 84 inches
152.4 x 213.4 cm

page 31
721 (The days' noise), 2016
Oil on linen
54 x 78 inches
137.2 x 198.1 cm

page 33
722 (Portage, noun or verb), 2016
Oil on linen
54 x 84 inches
137.2 x 213.4 cm

page 35
724 (Stammer, sidewalk), 2016
Oil on linen
66 x 48 inches
167.6 x 121.9 cm

page 37
725 (The sign says you are here), 2016
Oil on linen
30 x 22 inches
76.2 x 55.9 cm